OOKPIK

The Travels of a Snowy Owl

Bruce Hiscock

BOYDS MILLS PRESS
Honesdale, Pennsylvania

To the children of the Far North

The author wishes to thank Anne Hobbs, public information specialist, and Miyoko Chu, Ph.D., science editor, both with Cornell Lab of Ornithology, for their generous assistance.

Text and illustrations copyright © 2008 by Bruce Hiscock

Boyds Mills Press, Inc.
815 Church Street
Honesdale, Pennsylvania 18431
Printed in China

Library of Congress Cataloging-in-Publication Data

Hiscock, Bruce.
  Ookpik : the travels of a snowy owl / written and illustrated by Bruce Hiscock.—1st ed.
    p. cm.
  ISBN 978-1-59078-461-7 (hardcover : alk. paper)
  1. Snowy owl—Juvenile literature. 2. Snowy owl—Migration—Juvenile literature. I. Title.

  QL696.S83H57 2008
  598.9'7—dc22
                        2007017327

First edition
The text of this book is set in Times Roman.
The illustrations are done in watercolor and pencil on Arches paper.

10 9 8 7 6 5 4 3 2 1

INTRODUCTION

Owls have always been regarded as mysterious birds. They were thought of as omens in many societies, and owls are often pictured as the companions of wizards in folklore. Snowy owls, with their large yellow eyes and white feathers, seem special by any standard.

Snowy owls live in the Arctic and do not regularly migrate like geese. Each winter, however, a few snowy owls show up in southern Canada or the northern United States. When food supplies are low in the Arctic, larger numbers of these owls fly south. They are easy to spot, as they prefer to hunt in open lands like farm fields or major airports. News of a snowy owl sighting spreads quickly, and many people come to look.

The first snowy owl I ever saw was spending the winter in a field in northern New York State. The owl perched on hay bales, barns, and houses, but not in the trees at the edge of the field. That owl became the inspiration for this book. The story is as "true to life" as possible. I could not actually follow an owl on a journey like this. Instead, my writing relies on observations, research, and my own travels in the Arctic.

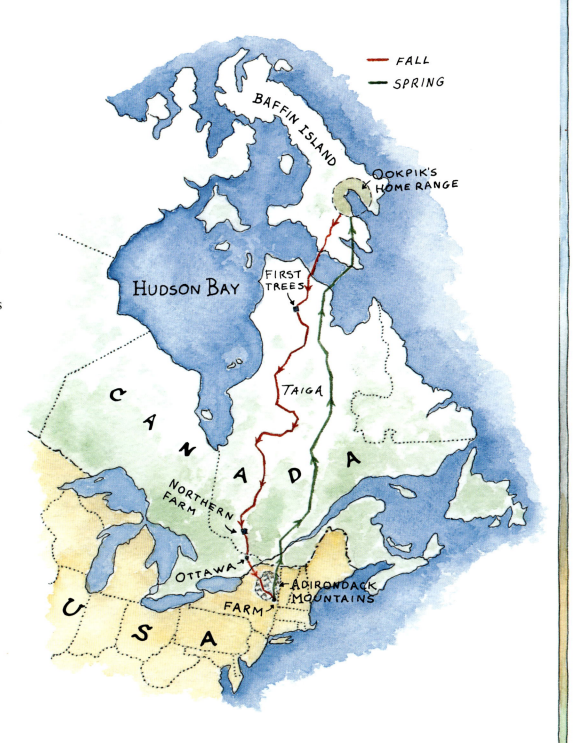

LEMMING

FOUR EGGS, WHITE AS THE SNOWS OF WINTER, lay in a shallow nest on the Arctic tundra. The eggs were still warm from the mother bird. But as gusts of icy wind swirled over them, they began to cool. An Arctic fox, making his rounds, saw the nest was left unguarded. He trotted straight up the hill, hoping to steal an egg or two.

Just as the fox was about to grab his prize, a huge white owl came streaking down from the sky. Feathered feet with sharp talons struck the little fox with a glancing blow. He tumbled backward, rolled over, and raced off.

With bright yellow eyes, the snowy owl examined each of her eggs. She saw they were untouched and settled down again on the nest. The north wind blew harder, but now the eggs were safe beneath the owl's thick feathers.

The snowy owl had been sitting on these eggs for a month. All during that time, her mate, a pure white male, brought her food. He was a good hunter. But lemmings, small furry rodents that are the favorite prey of snowy owls, were scarce that spring. The male owl was forced to chase after Arctic hares and small birds. They were far more difficult to catch than lemmings.

Scritch . . . scratch! A noise came from inside one of the eggs. Then a crack appeared in the shell. With more scratching and pecking, the egg broke open. A small, wet chick crawled out and hid beneath its mother.

Two days later, another egg hatched, and by the end of the week, four helpless, downy chicks huddled in the nest. The male owl ranged farther now, trying to find enough food for the family.

Children from a nearby village saw the white bird coming and going. "*Ookpik*!" they called, using the word for "snowy owl" in Inuktitut, the Inuit language. They were glad to see these owls were raising chicks. With few lemmings around, many snowy owls on Baffin Island would not nest at all that year.

Near the end of June, when the first chick was a week old, summer came to the tundra. It wasn't exactly hot, but flowers bloomed everywhere. The village children watched the mother owl from a distance. Her mate brought a small bird he had killed. She tore it up and gave pieces to the little owls. With beaks opened wide, they begged for more. The fuzzy white down on the oldest birds was changing to fuzzy gray as their feathers came in.

These days the mother seldom left the nest, for the chicks were not safe alone. Once, when she was away, a gull-like jaeger snatched a chick. The bird flew off quickly and fed the meat to its own babies.

During the next two weeks, the three remaining little owls left the nest and hid among the tundra grasses. They were growing fast but still unable to fly. The parents watched over them and brought them food. The big owls hunted in daylight, for during the brief Arctic summer, it is never dark.

Keeping the young owls fed was a struggle for the parents. Hunting far and wide, they were just able to find enough food. By early August, two of the owls were nearly full-grown, but the third chick had disappeared. Perhaps the fox had found it.

The oldest nestling was a male. He tested his wings frequently, hopping about and flapping. Then one blustery day, when the tufts of cotton grass bent low, he caught the wind. With a powerful stroke of his wings, he lifted up into the sky. It wasn't a long flight, but from that moment the owl was not a helpless bird on the ground. Now he was truly Ookpik, a snowy owl, a hunter able to fly.

Not long after that, his sister took her first flight, too. By the end of summer, they were hunting by themselves.

In the Far North, fall comes early. The leaves of the tiny blueberry bushes turn red, while the dwarf birch changes to yellow. Ducks, geese, gulls, and other birds begin leaving the land at this time. These migrating birds come north only for the nesting season. Snowy owls are true birds of the Arctic. Their feathers are exceptionally thick and warm, and they will stay on the tundra all year long if there is enough to eat.

The young male owl, Ookpik, had done fairly well so far. He found a few lemmings and had learned to hunt birds. Once, he caught a young Arctic hare. But now the days were rapidly growing shorter and much, much colder. Darkness had returned, and often the wind brought a dusting of snow. Without a steady supply of lemmings for food, the owl sensed that he must leave this place or die.

On a gray morning, Ookpik rose high above the tundra and headed south. For two days he flew on, hunting whatever he could find. Below the owl, the landscape began to change. Strange green plants appeared, sticking straight up from the ground. At first these plants were small, like standing children. But as the bird continued south, they became taller and stood closer together. The plants were trees, something new to the snowy owl.

Ookpik did not care for trees. He was accustomed to hunting the endless tundra where nothing blocked his view. When he found a treeless hillside, he landed on a lichen-covered rock. There he waited until his sharp eyes noticed something small scurrying in the field. He glided down, silent as death, and caught his first meadow vole. It was fat and much like a lemming.

For a time, the owl was satisfied to stay on the hill and hunt. But as the voles disappeared and the Arctic wind roared, he knew he must go farther south.

When Ookpik took to the air again, he could see nothing but trees below. This was the taiga, a great forest of black spruce and fir that covers the land south of the tundra. The sea of dark trees was broken only by frozen lakes and rivers. Other kinds of owls lived in this forest, but it was not a place for him. A snowy owl needs open land.

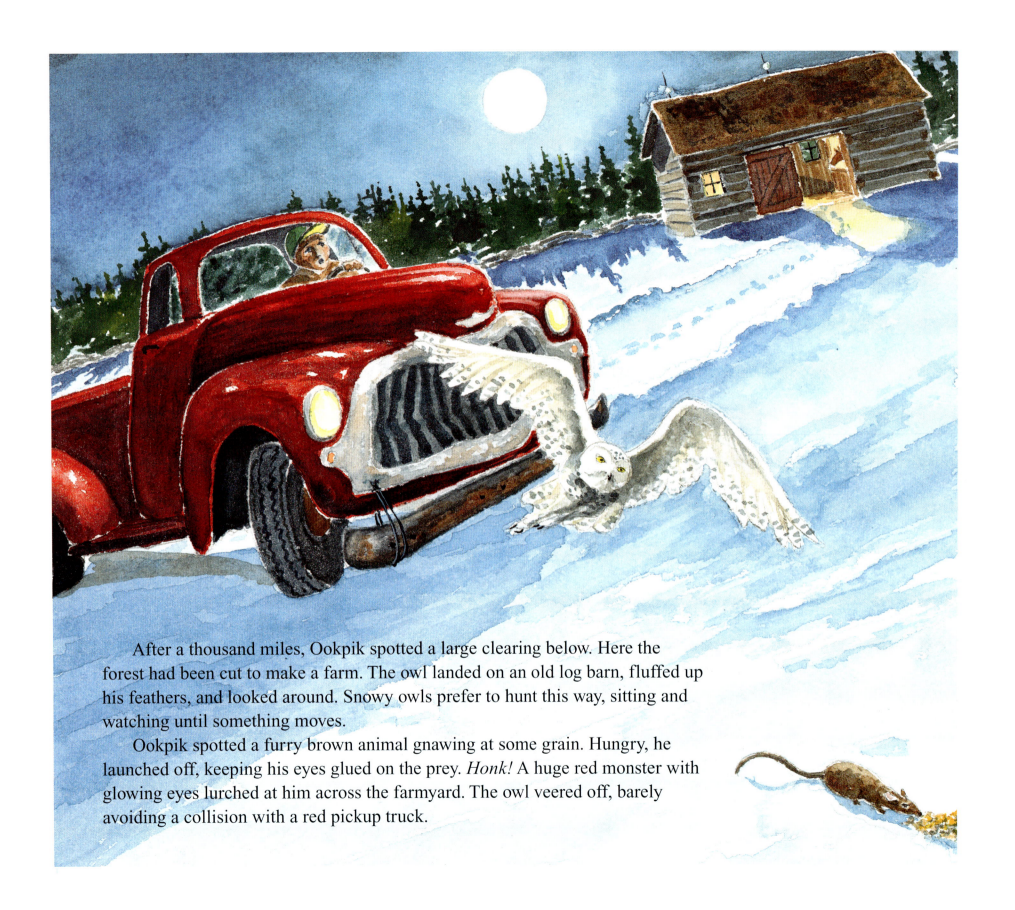

After a thousand miles, Ookpik spotted a large clearing below. Here the forest had been cut to make a farm. The owl landed on an old log barn, fluffed up his feathers, and looked around. Snowy owls prefer to hunt this way, sitting and watching until something moves.

Ookpik spotted a furry brown animal gnawing at some grain. Hungry, he launched off, keeping his eyes glued on the prey. *Honk!* A huge red monster with glowing eyes lurched at him across the farmyard. The owl veered off, barely avoiding a collision with a red pickup truck.

Once he learned to stay away from the truck, Ookpik found the farm was a wonderful place. There were plenty of mice and rats, and he was content to rest here from his long travels.

But after a week, a female snowy owl arrived. She was larger and older than he was. Snowy owls are very protective of their hunting territory. They like to have an area all to themselves, and so she chased Ookpik away.

He flew on, soaring over Ottawa, the capital of Canada. There, he saw pigeons roosting. Pigeons looked easy to catch, but the city was no place for a snowy owl. Ookpik continued south, and the next day he crossed into the United States.

With steady wing beats, Ookpik flew over the Adirondack Mountains. Few people lived here, but dense forest covered the steep slopes and broad valleys.

Beyond the mountains, he finally found the open space he needed. This was dairy-farm country. Huge pastures for cows and big fields where corn and hay had been harvested covered the land. The owl settled in for the winter. It wasn't quite like home, for there were still trees, but it would do. Tracks in the snow showed that mice and rabbits lived in these fields. And, compared with the Arctic, the cold did not seem severe.

When small birds, such as snow buntings, come south from the tundra, they often go unnoticed. Not so with a snowy owl. People driving by saw the big white bird sitting on a hay bale. The newspaper ran a story with a picture titled "Arctic Visitor." After that, many people wanted to see the white owl.

They came with binoculars, cameras, spotting scopes, and sometimes their neighbors. Ookpik was indifferent to his fame. The sight of this magnificent bird, however, thrilled the people. Everyone was warned not to approach too closely, and so the owl and the bird watchers got along well.

Most owls are rather secretive. They hunt by night and are hard to see. But Ookpik was usually in plain view, and he hunted any time he saw a small animal. In this way the winter months slipped by.

With the first warm days of spring, great flights of Canada geese winged over the farm, honking as they flew. Ookpik watched them and felt the pull of his birthplace. The winter had been good to him. He was strong, healthy, and ready for a long flight.

In bright daylight, the big owl left the meadows and started north. Stopping only to hunt, he flew over the mountains, over the cities and farms, and above the dark forests of the taiga.

After many days, the owl passed the land of little sticks, where small trees stand like children. Beyond those trees lay the hills and open plains of the Arctic. Here, at last, Ookpik was home. He glided down and landed on a tundra mound. The owl still had the dark spots of a young bird, for males do not become pure white until they are older.

"Ookpik!" shouted a girl from the village, and she ran to tell her friends. The snowy owl paid no attention. He sat perfectly still, waiting for the first lemming to appear.

RANGE

Snowy owls are found in the northernmost lands all around the world. This includes Alaska, Canada, Greenland, Iceland, some British Isles, Scandinavia, and Russia, including Siberia. They are able to survive in the Arctic because their thick feathers provide what is perhaps the best insulation of any bird in the world. Even their feet are well feathered.

SIZE

Snowy owls are big birds. They are the second-largest North American owl, just behind the great gray owl. Snowy owls are about two feet long (61 centimeters) from head to tail, with a wingspan of around five feet (152 centimeters). Adults weigh in the neighborhood of four pounds (1.8 kilograms). Females are slightly larger than males.

FOOD

The primary food of most snowy owls is the lemming. These hamster-sized rodents do not hibernate but remain active all year long. In winter, they live in a maze of tunnels under the snow and nibble on tundra plants.

The number of lemmings in any area varies greatly, usually in four-year cycles. At the peak of the cycle, lemmings are everywhere. Snowy owls will lay many eggs and raise many chicks when lemmings are plentiful. Tundra vegetation is slow growing, however, and cannot support massive numbers of lemmings for very long. As a result, many lemmings die at this point of the cycle, sometimes drowning in rivers or the ocean as they try to swim to new territory. When this happens, the lemming population is said to "crash."

The next year, when lemmings are scarce, snowy owls will lay fewer eggs or skip nesting altogether. When I was in the Arctic National Wildlife Refuge in Alaska in 1998, there were no lemmings to be seen, only their deserted tunnels. And there were no snowy owls either, just feathers and owl pellets near grassy mounds on the tundra.

Owl pellets are the remains of animals the owl has eaten. Like all owls, snowy owls eat lemmings, mice, and other small rodents whole and headfirst. Later, the indigestible bones and fur are coughed up in a marble-sized owl pellet.

When feeding new chicks, owl parents tear the prey apart. Snowy owls feed a sort of "fillet of lemming," pieces of meat mostly free of fur and bones, to their newly hatched young. The owls grow quickly. The parents need to supply about two lemmings a day for each chick until the young owls can hunt on their own.

COURTSHIP AND NESTING

Snowy owls begin courting in March and April. The male owls fly in wavy patterns. This presumably impresses the females. The males will also catch a lemming and present it to the females, showing they are good providers. Snowy owls mate only for the season. In very good lemming years, some males have been known to have two mates, both with nests, at the same time!

The nest is just a shallow scrape in the ground, sometimes lined with plants or feathers. It is usually on a high place and must be close to a good hunting ground. Eggs are laid in about two-day intervals, beginning in May. They are close to the size of large chicken eggs and are pure white. The female might lay as many as fifteen eggs in a year when lemmings are plentiful, but seven or eight eggs is about average. In a year when food is hard to find, there will be fewer eggs or none.

The female begins sitting on each egg as soon as it is laid. Since the eggs depend on warmth and time for development, they will hatch in the order that they were laid. After about thirty-three days, the first egg hatches, followed by the others in two-day intervals. This means the first chick can be quite a bit older than the last chick. This helps ensure that at least some of the chicks will survive. In a year when lemmings are plentiful, most, sometimes all, of the chicks will live. Foxes and other predators will not bother a snowy owl nest if they have plenty of lemmings to eat. They recognize that owls are powerful birds and will defend their nests vigorously. Other birds, such as ducks and geese, sometimes build nests near the snowy owl's nest, knowing that the owl will keep predators away.

LIFE

Little owls are covered with fluffy white down for the first week or so after they hatch. Gray down appears as their feathers begin to grow in. They leave the nest when they are three to four weeks old, but these chicks still cannot fly. Leaving the nest is a survival strategy. The chicks spread out and hide among the tundra plants. By separating in this way, it is unlikely that every small owl will be found by foxes, wolves, or birds of prey. If they stayed together, a predator might take the entire brood. The fledglings begin flying when they are about fifty days old and can fly nearly as well as their parents after a week or two.

Like most wild birds, about half of the nestlings will not live through the first year. Predators, lack of food, and bad weather all take a toll. If an owl makes it through the first year, its chances of surviving the next years are much better.

In the wild, snowy owls usually mate when they are two years old and can live to be ten. In zoos, snowies have lived for over thirty years.

Snowy owls are true birds of the Arctic. Scientists studying global warming have noted that the loss of sea ice and permafrost indicates the Arctic climate is changing more rapidly than in other locations. What effect this will have on these magnificent white birds is not yet known.

LEMMING